AF650962

A MOMENT WITHOUT DIMENSION

A Collection of Poems

ANJALI PATWARDHAN

Creative CROWS
PUBLISHERS LLP
the publishing & communication people

Published by

Creative CROWS
PUBLISHERS LLP
the publishing & communication people

Office: A-42, Dayanand Colony,

New Delhi(South)-110024

Mobiles: +91-9953758404, +91-9833283155

Emails: ganivpanjrath@yahoo.co.in, tannaazirani@gmail.com

Copyright © 2021, Anjali Patwardhan

No part of the book may be reproduced, stored in a retrieval system, or transmitted in any form by any means, electronic, mechanical, photocopying, recording or otherwise, without the prior written permission from the publishers. The views, content and opinion expressed in the book are the individual assertion and opinion of the author and the publisher does not take any responsibility for the same in any manner whatsoever. The same shall solely be the responsibility of the author.

Disclaimer

This book is a work of fiction and any resemblance to actual persons living or dead is purely coincidental.

ISBN-13: 978-93-91526-12-2

ISBN 10: 93-91526-12-8

MRP: ₹ 325/-

Printed and bound by Creative Crows Publishers LLP, New Delhi

Contents

I Dedicate This Book to You

A Note of Thanks

I thank each one of you, who inspire me every day. Who make me want to write better. Who make me want to be a better me.

Preface

Memories are timeless. We cannot hope to fit them in any box or dimension. We all carry them in our hearts and our minds. Some bring us tears, some joy. Some we wish we could re-live again and some, we would rather forget. Memories make a home within us. They are, our treasure trove. Through these poems, I share with all of you, a part of me.

Foreword

"Time does not change us. It just unfolds us." - Max Frisch

And this was the first thought that struck me when I sat down to read your poems, Anjali. Before sitting down to write the Foreword for your second collection, I decided to revisit the first collection and I could actually visualize your journey through the poems: your journey from a young girl to a beloved to a mother to now a Woman in her own right-comfortable in her own skin.

Time has actually unfolded you from a fledgling poet to one who is more assured in her choice of words and imagery; one who is bold in her choice of themes. One noticeable feature of your writing is that through all your poems runs a common thread of deep and sensitive connect with nature- it is as if Nature is your Muse and it holds your soul in its palm tenderly, like a firefly.

Apart from Nature, another recurring theme, in this collection, is that of silence-

the unspoken, the unheard- "your voice I strain to listen to", "And the waves on the shore, calling her again", "For they could hear the words unsaid", Can you hear me sing you a lullaby?"- are just a few examples.
And so the conversation goes on with some things said and some left unsaid through the poems so well-crafted with love and care.

Happy reading!!!
Kavita Rana
Educationist
(My school teacher)

Foreword

Having known Anjali since we were children, it came to me as no surprise when she announced the release of her first book of poetry. Now on her second one, which is even more profound, she has surpassed herself not just in the skill of writing poetry but also in the projection of her thoughts and innermost feelings. What I find most fascinating about Anjali's poetry is the spectrum of subjects she touches upon; it could be a kaleidoscope of feelings arising out of observing her surroundings or intense expressions of the matters of the heart.

A lazy afternoon, or a vacation by the sea side, a brooding evening or a Sunday morning coffee, Anjali's poetry I would call an 'any time read' - easy to understand and relatable. Her pages leave you with a lingering feeling of wanting more, each time you keep the book down.

Rashmi Joshi

*Author of books – **'Here and Beyond'** and **'Men-Women, Mars-Venus & All That B***S***'**; working on the third one titled,*

'Patanjali Yogasutra's - Where Science and Spirit Meet'.

A Post Graduate in HR, a Master's Degree holder in Labour Law, an Ayush certified level 3 yoga trainer, and an erstwhile classical singer.

Foreword

Anjali reminds me of a natural mountain stream - melodious, giving, full of life and refreshing.
I have met Anjali on a few occasions, mostly poetry meets, and every time I have seen a different facet of her pleasant self. Earlier it was her simplicity and smile, and then came some naughty comments and child-like giggles, and sometimes deep understandings of life and love.
I realise the same is reflected in her poems. Some are so romantic, some are so innocent and some happily naughty.

I find effortless flowing quality in her writings. Maybe it is because she doesn't write to fill a void or to make a statement; she just writes. It's her connection with her universe.
In her own words:
Words and I go hand in hand
Like the tall oak tree, with a green vine entwined

Read her poems aloud, let them seep into you and touch your core. You will smile, laugh, shed a tear, remember a loved one and connect with yourself.

You hold me close
And for a fleeting moment
Something magical happens
And we become one

This is the magic that Anjali brings to our world.

I often tell her 'the universe needs more poets like you.'

My honest, happy, loving wishes to my Angel for her –"A ***moment without dimension****".*

Sonali Rasal
A poet at heart, Landscape Architect & Environmental Consultant by profession and Founder of Literature Club: The Corinthians Literati in Pune.

Foreword

*I have seen Anjali undertake the journey from '**Unfrozen Wings**' to '**A moment without dimension**', and I can proudly say that she has churned out yet another masterpiece!*
Her poems have a freshness in them, which can be smelt...a lilting melody which can be heard with closed eyes and emotions that never fail to warm your heart!
The simplicity of words make them relatable and she weaves them with elegance... as if stringing petite flowers into a delicate garland.

Mamata Hiremath
MA (Clinical Psychology), PGD (School Psychology), Clinical Hypnotherapist (Past Life Regression)

Till Eternity

I will paint you with my love
As you stand before me
And hold your hands, for as long as I live
And that my love,
"Is till eternity"

The Days Forever

The days were always sunny and bright
Bougainville's pink waving in my sight.....
The gate always open
The picket fence never too high.......
The days never too warm
The nights never too cold.....
The monsoons never too rainy
The sky never too dark........
The road never too long
T'was a run in the grass
A roll down a hill
The beautiful laughter, down the decades
The cheerful face cheering me till now
Never stopping, never tiring
A moment without a dimension
Defines, a memory.

An Ode to My Words

Words and I go hand in hand
Like the tall oak tree, with a green vine entwined
We share an untold story, which only our hearts know
But I think the time is right, to let the whole world know

You walked into my life
When I needed you the most
You gave me a shoulder to lean on
A strong steady hold

You cleared up the clouds
Which were pouring on me
And gave way to sweet sunshine
Which opened, a new chapter for me

Each day dawned with the colour of love
And kept on getting sweeter
Like the beautiful flowers' nectar,
I need no more, only you by my side
Words and only words, to keep me shining bright.

Celebrating Us

I am a whiff, of the most fragrant perfume
That keeps lingering close by
Drawing towards me, the love of my life

My touch is like a feather
As soft as a new born's cheeks,
My kiss is like a rose petal
Caressing your face
Making you smile, like sweet sunshine

So surround me with your love
For that is the only thing I will ever need
Gather me in your arms
For that, is where I truly belong

Surround me with our love song
For that is the most mesmerising melody
Sweep me off my feet
So I can tell you, that I love you

We are the most perfect pair
For one is tears, the other smiles
We make the most beautiful pair
For one is rain, the other sunshine

It is forever, that I am yours and you are mine
So let us renew our vows at sunset,

And see the morning sunrise, with a tinge of crimson, celebrating our love
Till the horizon is in sight.

Eternal Bliss

In the confines of my bedroom
My comfort zone,
I still find your presence
And know, we are forever, meant to be

So sing with me, as I sing for you
Dance with me, as I tiptoe on your toes
Gather me in your arms and look into my eyes
For they speak only one name, and that name is you

Follow me as I take the lead
And take you to a sacred, secret place
That is filled with love and only love
In my heart, is where you will always stay

Listen to the unspoken words from my lips
For they yearn to kiss you and hold you in my embrace
And if that, is eternal bliss,

I want time to stop and take a break,
To let me love you and hold your hand,
To be there for you,
As your one, true soul mate.

Home

Under the cascading rain
The rainbow rays
The moonlight stream
The morning sun's beam
Under the shadow of the tree
Its beautiful leaves
Those breath-taking flowers
And most of all, the soothing breeze

I wait for you
Each moment of the day
I wait for you
To call my name
I wait to catch a glimpse of you
I wait for you to look my way

The waiting ends, and the spotlight is on us
There...it's only you and I
Waltzing through the night
On top of the highest mountain peak
Down magical forest floors

And before we know,
It's dawn, and the twinkling stars fall asleep
The music, a faint whisper in the distant
The moon smiling, waiting to go into hiding

It is pin drop silence now,
When the birds start chirping
And as we stand there and hold each other
In a warm, tender embrace
We find what we have always wanted,
A safe haven,
And we know for sure, that we have finally found a place we have been longing for...
Home.

Sweet Sunshine

That beautiful colour of sweet sunshine
Glowing on your skin
As though the sun's first rays
Were trying to find you...
And there you were
Lying on the floor
Covered with green grass
And tiny dew drops,
When they lay their rays on you
Making you sparkle
Like the most precious diamond...
You woke up with a glow in your eyes
And all because, you are my sweet sunshine.

Butterfly

My heart… beats, as it speaks
Like a fluttering butterfly
Its wings itching to fly
The world outside seemed so blue
Let me take, my first flight

The sun was rising in the distant
The birds were chirping in the midst
The flowers bloomed
The dew drops glistened

"What a beautiful world," the butterfly thought
Let me go searching
A faint sound of sweet music
Humming, in its delicate ears

"Time to go home now," the butterfly exclaimed
For a new day to dawn…
A beautiful melody is in the making
Let's strum, the right notes now.

Musical Notes

A single note
That is all it takes
Oh! That one note of music
To stir my soul so deep within

Out of nowhere I have a teardrop in my eye
How? I didn't even come to know
Perhaps it awoke some long lost memories
And opened a door into the known
Which was, until then, still unknown to me

I looked deep inside
But it took a while before I realised
That there always was
A lyrical, playing within me

I saw myself surrounded by those musical notes
And into a trance I went
Playing the whole night long

Only when the chirping of the birds did I hear,
I opened my eyes to a beautiful sunrise
Its rays straining to get to me
To ask me to play another melody

The sky lit up and a rainbow I saw
With the words I was singing
And the notes I was strumming

For a moment, time, stood still
And I saw myself tearing up again
Coz somewhere within
As I strained to listen
I heard the note all over again
Asking me to close my eyes
So it could teach me what it was
To be myself...... yet again.

Realms of Time

Will you hold me tonight
And pluck them clouds for me
So I could see the silver lining
To pick up a few stars for you and me

I will wish upon them
And send them on their way
So many eons later
I would find them come my way

They would tell me all
About you and I
And all the memories locked in them
Revealing themselves one at a time

Knowing, that you and I
Have always crossed each other's path
Brings me joy like no other
And a look on my face, that takes, even my
breath away

Let us always be together, forever, my dear
And bring each other happiness and cheer
Belonging, that has no boundaries
And love in our hearts, which will beat, forever and ever.

An Enigma That Is You

What is it about you?
That makes my heart skip a beat,
Probably the unspoken, you want to speak
with me

What is it about you?
That every time I think of you,
My eyes well up with joy
And I want to sing a song
Only for you

What is it about you?
That is so endearing,
That every time I see you
I want to love you, in a hundred different
ways

What is it about you?
That is so beautiful,
That smile on your lips
And a twinkle in your eyes
Whenever you talk to me

What is it about you?
That is so appealing,
The way you make me feel
A woman and a child, both, in one go

What is it about you?
That is so admirable,
The way you treat everyone
With kindness and cheer

What is it about you?
That makes you so exceptional,
It's just the way you carry yourself
With so much ease and a charming grace

What is it about you?
That I love so much,
You cherish me in a way
That you know, I truly deserve

So let me hold you close
And let you forever know
That I will always be with you
Walking hand in hand
Till an endless possible time.

Unspoken Words

When you sit with me after a long tiring day
Holding my hands wanting me to stay
Waiting for me to patiently listen
To what is it that you have to say

Not a word transpires
Coz just by looking at you
I can see your eyes convey
All that is on your mind
And all that is faraway

I caress your lips with my fingertips
Taking in your beautiful face
Those sensuous alluring eyes
And your lovely winsome smile

You hold me close
And for a fleeting moment
Something magical happens
And we become one
In spirit and in oneness
Looking at each other
With love and tenderness

Need anything more be said
Than the words, I love you
For they say it all and more
Between the lines, a language unto themselves
Which both of us can perfectly unfold.

Finding Myself

I see myself falling,
Into the crevices
Even I didn't know existed

And as I fall through
I see the light disappear,
I am surrounded by darkness
But there is nothing to fear

For I sense a presence
Which had been long waiting
For me to find my way,
Way back to my origin...

I then saw a vision
Crystal clear and just so pure
Of me... laughing and giggling
Like the small child that I really am

As I picked her up
And hugged her close to me,
I became alive
In a sense, that was new to me

A heart to heart I had with her
And she listened, so patiently
All she did was hear me out
Then whispered in my ears quietly

"Don't always keep me in hiding
Make me seen,
Make me heard,
It sometimes gets ever so lonely,
So make some time to come and meet me"

In the blink of an eye
Darkness gave way to an illuminated pathway
And I seemed to find myself
Under a shower of dazzling stars descending from above

As I woke up to a new morning
To the sound of raindrops
Singing my favourite song,
All I wished for,
Is to go back into the crevices
Where I could find myself, all over again.

Silence

In the silence that engulfs me
Now that you are gone
I sit quietly, waiting for the calm to take over me
So I can start a conversation with you
Wherever you may be

In the times when I feel lonely and lost
It is your voice I strain to listen to
Waiting for you to send me a message
From here and beyond

You always knew the right words to say
You always knew how to comfort me, in your own sweet way
You always did everything, with so much poise and an unmatched grace

I miss your presence in my life
And though you are always by my side
I wish I could hold your hand just one more time
I wish I could see you by my side just one more time
I wish you would make everything just right

Come, be with me, whenever you have the time
So I can hold you in my embrace
Freeze time,
And be together, till time infinite.

Cry of The Soul

When I won't wake up to a new tomorrow
A beautiful day that was only mine to take
Don't cry, for I was not strong enough
To take the pain and go along the way
Deep down everything seemed so hollow
Was I even real, was a question that followed

I am, but just a tiny speck in this vast universe
So I won't be missed, for there are too many stars dancing in the night sky
Which are way more bright, that seem to dim my light
It's time for me to exit
My time is done,
So let me make way
For a new day, a new sunrise and a brand new sunset for me to see, through my beloved's eyes.

The Fallen Tree

She wondered what was wrong with her
And realised, she was as insignificant as the fallen tree
Not a second glance
Not a second chance
Just fade and vanish away
Never to be found
Never to be seen
Maybe, just maybe
To be reminisced an odd day
When the wind can't find its way
And it stops and waits,
Sheds a tear in silence
And goes along its way
Gone were the days
When she was all anyone ever wanted
Now, a distant memory, just a memory
As insignificant, as the fallen tree.

Quest for Acceptance

I don't really fit in any box
Nor do I fit in any mould
I am just a wanderer
Seeking...
To be a part of the unfinished puzzle
But I don't fit in there too...
I am, but only a dream
And that is where I shall remain
In the closet, in the cupboard, behind closed doors
And that is where, I truly belong.

Soothing the Broken Heart

When your heart is broken
And it bleeds
It cries out for help,
All I want to do,
Is to hold it tenderly
Wipe away the tears
And caress it gently

When your heart is broken
And wants to go back in time
The time when it was innocent
Harsh words just brushed passed by
For they didn't mean a dime

When your heart is broken
All it wants
Is a kind heart
To mend it
To make it whole
So it can beat
With the same love and compassion it once did

When your heart is broken
And doesn't know what to do
All I want to do,

Is to gather it in my arms
And mend the broken pieces

When your heart is broken
And doesn't know who to turn to
All I want to do
Is talk to it
And say you are not alone

When your heart is broken
All it is asking for, is compassion, warmth, acceptance and empathy
And maybe an angel
To gently hold its hand
Protect it and guide it through life's journey

When your heart is broken
All that it wants
Is love,
That will stand through testing times
And keep it together
To weather all that comes it way
And make it a little easy
So it can get through the day.

If Not for You

What would I be?
If not for you
What would I seek?
If not for you
Who would I breathe?
If not for you
Who would I feel?
If not for you
What would I be grateful for?
If not for you
Who would I look forward to?
If not for you
Who would I search for happiness with?
If not for you
Who would I live for?
If not for you
Who would I go on life's adventures with?
If not for you
Who would be my safe haven?
If not for you
Who would I love and cherish?
If not for you
Who would be my one true soul mate?
If not for you.

You and Me

You looked at me
And I started to blush
Making me feel special
Wanting, only love in return

We smiled at each other
And conveyed what was on our lips
Loving each other
Without telling another

"I wish to grow old with you," you told me once
I wish upon it, as soon as the day begins
I wish you and I, in every breath I ever take
I wish us all the happiness and joy
That is truly ours to take.

My Dreams for You

I want to sit with you on the highest mountain peak
Down golden sandy beaches,
Traverse through the realms of time
And tell you all my dreams

I want you to smell the rain
As it falls slowly on your beautiful face
Caressing you, making you smile
Wanting to embrace you and give you, the gift of time

I want you to smell the flowers
As they open up each sunny morn
Taking you back in time
Reminding you, of just how enchanting you are

I want you to listen to the wind
As it whispers in your ears
And kisses your beautiful lips
Letting you know, that I have sent them for you

I want you to let the butterflies sit on you
And dance in your embrace
For they want you to know
This is where they feel, most safe

I want you to know
What I sometimes never say
You are my blessing, my sunshine
Who wipes the gloomy clouds away

There will always be so much more to what I want to say,
Sit with me one starry night
When the moon is shining bright
Up upon the meadows so high
So I can tell you all, before, its sunrise.

Innocence of The Heart

Sat down to write
What's on my mind
Went blank in a flash of light
Oh! Why can't I get anything right?

What should I do, I ask myself
Sing a song or pen down my thoughts
Give a little shake to my everyday life
Or be bold and confident and take charge
of my flight

Soar high, fly low
Climb up, walk down
Take in the joy of the present I know
Or hum a little rhyme of my future in tow

Whatever I do
I will follow my heart
For my destiny is waiting
With open arms in my thought.

Symphony of Melodies

The song was hidden deep within
The depths of the ocean
As she strained to listen

One by one, the notes came up
Oh! What a melody she sang,
Was a treat to listen

A soft, soothing voice crooned through the night
The waves glistened,
And the stars shone bright

The sun was waiting to rise again
But the moon refused to go away
For he wanted to hold on to those precious moments
When he could sway behind the clouds
And sing, in his own sweet way

Finally it dawned
And the sun came up,
The early morning sunrays
Creating ripples on the waves

*Time to go home now, the notes exclaimed
And rise above, when in darkness, "The
Voice" called to them again.*

Hope

I long to watch each sunrise with you
And the gorgeous sunsets too
Holding hands
As I walk in your footsteps
That you just imprinted on the cold, beautiful grainy sand

I will pick up all the delicate, differently shaped shells lying on the beach
And make a wind chime for the door,
So every time that you walk in
My heart will flutter with joy

I will capture all the hues in the sky
And paint a picture for you to see
Of the different shades of our love
Some yellow, some orange, some heavenly crimson too

I will let you in where nobody has been
And keep you there forever
Living my life like a dream come true
Under the open blue skies
Basking in your love
In your eternally, loving embrace.

Serendipity

The sea was singing, in tune with the winds
The seagulls were about to call it a day,
The setting sun, getting ready to sleep
And the waves on the shore, calling her again

And there she was, sitting on the seashore
Looking at the horizon, humming a song
The gentle breeze kissing her lips
Bringing a smile, which they had truly missed

Through the mist she saw a silhouette
A beautiful vision, just as she had envisioned

He sat down beside her
And wrapped his arms around her,
She looked at him
As their eyes met,
No words were needed
For they could hear the words unsaid

He caressed her face
As a tear drop fell,
He wiped it away, and held her close instead

They sat by the seashore, for a little while longer
In silence, as they always had
Always finding each other
At the right, propitious moment.

Can You Hear Me?

Can you hear me?
In the drizzle of the rain
When the raindrops fall on your windowpane

Can you hear me sing?
When the flowers wake up
Trying to let the sunshine in

Can you hear me laugh?
When the breeze is knocking on your door
Wanting to caress your sweet innocent face

Can you hear me sing you a lullaby?
When you try to sleep
On a warm summer day

Can you feel me hug you?
When the winter chill makes you shiver
And in an instant, warmth takes over

Can you feel me kiss you?
The moment you think of me
Hoping I was standing close by
So you could peck my rosy lips

Can you feel me love you?
Coz, wherever you go,
You only see me
And know in your heart
That we were always meant to be.

Shining Star

As the sun set last night
A star was about to complete its life
A life full of ups and downs
But always shining bright

Each night that the star came out
Out of its hiding, shouting out loud
With renewed glory and a new found flame
Looking for friends and family to play

A picnic on the rainbow
High tea in the meadows
A cup of coffee on the snow-capped mountains
And sound sleep on forest trees

Each night ended
Exactly how I had seen,
When I see the star shine bright
Only for me.

Guiding Angel

She sat by the window
With a lone candle in her hands
Guarding the light
So it would show the way
To the wandering soul
Who didn't know, which way to go

She sat all night
Safeguarding the candle
So the wanderer could reach home
Safe and sound
Unscathed and unharmed

At the crack of dawn as she got up
The beautiful sun rays streamed through the clouds
That's when she knew her work was done
And a flock of birds
Sat on her windowsill
Crooning the sweetest music
A thank you note,
From the wandering soul

She smiled to herself
As she got about the day
Knowing, she would be right there
Guiding the lone wanderer,
Whenever he needed her, to show him the
way.

Red Lipstick

If you were the smile on my lips,
I would look in the mirror and put on some red lipstick
Put on some kohl around my eyes
Dance in the rain
And look up at the sky

Wonder in amazement, what I did, to have you in my life
And there I would see you, walk towards me
I would wait for you to take me in your arms
And share a passionate kiss, full of love

I would get all starry eyed
And you would give me your most enchanting smile
I would be speechless,
For that was enough......

And as I would reach for the red lipstick again
I would look in the mirror
And search for your smile, which I know, is forever mine.

Love's Embrace

As I bask in the embrace of your love
The love you have only for me
The eyes that speak only the truth
Saying, that you cherish me

I have only words and nothing more to gift
Until I meet you tomorrow
And a kiss is what I will give

A hug so tight, I won't let you breathe
My fingers caressing your face
Your eyes, taking all in

Just keep me in a tiny little corner of your heart
That you come home to each day
Talk to me, share with me
What you wanted to say whole day

When you call it a day
Light a little candle and see me by your side
Loving you like no other,
Patting you to sleep, in my ever warm embrace.

You, Me and A Cup of Coffee

You made me a cup of coffee
With a dash of love,
A hint of cinnamon,
Some fairy dust,
And your magic touch

You stood gazing
Trying to fathom
What was happening to me
As I took a sip of the coffee
You gave me, so lovingly

Couldn't you just see it my darling
It was love,
Only love
The one that has travelled through the realms of time
And now needed to be opened, as a present, by you and I

As your fingers brushed passed my lips
I shivered and tingled within
You gently tucked my lock of hair behind my ears
And hugged me, so I would know that you loved me so

Tender, sweet loving moments we shared
I wish I could rewind time and live them again

We complement each other
Like a beautiful poem,
As you whisper the words and I complete the verse

So darling, make me another cup of coffee will you
And let the magic begin
So I can fall in love with you
To open the present and live the wonder, all over again.

Tell Me Your Dreams

Through the trees I saw the sunrise
And walked on the beach, that beautiful morn
Its reflection, falling on the sand
Giving a golden shimmer, to all that touched my hand
The cold sand, the cool water, the gentle sea breeze, those tiny dainty shells
And my sweetheart, walking with me

Waves caressing my feet
Coaxing me, to tell them my dreams
My deepest desires that they saw within
Asking me to spell them out, so they could make them come true
For you and me

I confided everything and more
And kept on talking till it was night
The waves quietly went by
Conveying to each other, to never leave my side

At last when I looked around
Saw myself surrounded in my own little paradise
Fireflies to light up my living room
Beautiful, delicate, iridescent butterflies adorning my bedroom
Pitter patter of raindrops to wake me up
The sound of the waves to get me through the day
And the sparkling, twinkling stars, singing my favourite song

I could live like this forever I say
As I held your hands and danced and swayed
Looking forward to a brand new dawn
And to living my life, just the way I want.

My Valentine

When I think of you
Morning, noon and night
I want to caress your beautiful face
And look into those precious eyes,
I want to go deep within them
And see what is inside
To see what makes you so special
My sweet valentine

I want to know what keeps your heart beating
What is it, that it is still searching?
Its rhythm so melodious
That I could keep on listening

I want to know the secret behind your smile
The precious curve on your beautiful lips
That I wish to plant a kiss on them
Each time, I see you in my mind

I love you, with all my heart
And I know I always will
I love you, for who you are
And you make me shine, my sweet valentine.

Until I Met You

Didn't know what love was
Until I met you
Didn't know what belonging was
Until I met you
Didn't know what heart skipping a beat was
Until I met you
Didn't know what caring unconditionally was
Until I met you
Didn't know what longing was
Until I met you
Didn't know what acceptance was
Until I met you
Didn't know I was worth anything at all
Until I met you
Didn't know I mattered to anyone
Until I met you
Didn't know what life was
Until I met you
Didn't know what destiny was
Until I met you

Now I know all, and much more
All because, I met you.

Mom

It was just yesterday, when she first held you in her arms
It was just yesterday, when she taught you to take your first step
It was just yesterday, when she taught you your first word
It was just yesterday, when her eyes welled up seeing you go to school, for the very first time
It was just yesterday, when she held her head high, when she was known as your MOM
It was just yesterday, when she made a man out of the boy you were
It was just yesterday, when she knew her job was done
It was just yesterday, when God wanted her, needed her to be a guiding angel for more people than just you
It was just yesterday, when she knew she had done her best
It was just yesterday, when she said her final goodbye...

So today, the brightest star shining in the night sky, is her
As she protects you, looks after you, guides you,
And makes it a little easier for you,
To get through, your toughest days.

The Beginning, As It Ends

It's over
They pulled the plug
It's over
They signed on the dotted line
It's over
They said goodbye
It's over
As tears, welled up in their eyes

What went wrong?

Did she say too much...
Did he say too little...
Did she do too much...
Did he do too little...
Did he want too much...
Did she give too little...

In this tussle,
They forgot too much
And cared too little

What went wrong?
They tried to fathom
How did it not workout, baffled the others
What seemed so perfect
Was not to be
We, mere spectators in the amphitheatre
Trying to comprehend, what was unravelling?

The end just came
With a blink of an eye
Everything just scattered in pieces lying by
Death was knocking at the door
Not to snub away a life
But shatter the thin glass
Only they knew, how to tread on

Pin drop silence
Still, deathly still
The feeling, of "a life" crossing over

And then the calm, a whisper of hope
Cool breeze, sweet chattering trees
The warm rising sun
And somewhere, a note, of a promise being sung

Indeed every cloud has a silver lining,
So go find yours
And engulf yourself in that warm feeling

Sit in the beautiful silence surrounding you,
And count your blessings,
As they are being showered upon you.

Blank Pages

Crisp white beautiful pages
Lay in the drawer
Whispering amongst themselves
It's been a while she wrote on us
Where in the world could she be?

Is she okay?
Is she fine?
Is she in any distress?
If only there was a way to find

Day and night for days together
They waited with bated breath
That the drawer would open
And she would lovingly hold them in her hands
Sing a little,
And write on them, like she always had

They conspired together to send her a message
And tell her they were missing the words
The ones she wrote on them through the night
Under the stars and beautiful moonlight
For her words gave them life

Took them on journeys and places
Which on their own, they would never find

Their wait was finally over
When, in the middle of the night
A key turned and the drawer opened
The pages hustled and woke up with a smile
Jumping with joy and excitement
Knowing.....
Soon enough they would be filled with words, amazing stories and enchanting poetry

And sure enough, before the night was over,
One by one she filled the pages
They all blossomed and came alive
Did a sweet little dance, at being granted a new life

By morning she was all done
And she sat thinking on her chair
She would be back and not stay away
From her crisp white pages
Which had been kept in waiting, for an endless possible time.

One Winter's Day

By the stream she walked one winter's day
A rickety road along the way
Thick bushes on either side
And gorgeous wild flowers beaming at the sky

The water crystal clear
As blue as her eyes and sparkling clear
Colourful stones and pebbles she saw
Some green, some grey, some earthy browns

Looking around her enchanting surroundings
She chanced upon a quaint little bridge
The closer she went
Her heart did a flutter
For next to the bridge was a charming cottage

What a picturesque and heart-warming place she felt
And sat down on the luscious green grass with a plop,
To take upon this hiding place
For no one had ever seen it, up until today

Ducks in the water, quacking all along
The chirping birds, singing a song
Butterflies a dozen, sitting on the flowers
The bees in plenty, buzzing all around

Looking to the heavens above
She saw tall pine trees kissing the sky
She lay down and closed her eyes
Took in the heavenly smells and smiled

She woke up and missed a heartbeat
For there in front of her was a family of deer
They came close to her
Nudged her to come along
For in her they found a friend, from far and beyond

She took in one last time
Her ethereal surroundings
Where she could make a home some day

She made a promise to come back soon
And live in this place, known as heaven on earth
For as long as she wanted to stay.

Blessings

In the early hours of the morning,
I woke up to a sound
To the sound of bells ringing,
And a mystic voice speaking

The voice was so mesmerising
That I was drawn to it
Like a ship to sea

I sat in the audience
And felt a blessing come my way
And knew in that instant
This is where I was meant to stay

In blissfulness, in peace, in tune with myself
Never to falter and go the wrong way
Or fall and hurt myself ever again

To surrender myself to the universe
Never question or have a doubt
That it will always give me, what I need
In abundance and grace.

Olive Green

Chiffons or georgettes
Pearls or precious stones
High heels or simple flats
Ladies meet or a welfare eve
Coffee morning or a special meet
Countless occasions come into my life
Many hats and roles I adorn
But the one that fills me with joy and pride
Is being "**The Olive Wife**"

I missed no one back home
For I was welcomed with open arms
And made to feel at home
From a shy girl I grew leaps and bounds
Into a beautiful woman
A woman of substance
A woman, with a heart of gold

Be it a peace or a field posting
My better half made me so strong
That I could now handle anything
For I was now ready, to face any storm

Parent teacher meets or annual functions
A visit to the dentist or the magic show
Many a times I went alone
For my knight in shining armour
Was manning, the unformidable fort

In the end, what matters is the pride
The joy I have, seeing him by my side
To walk alongside him one step at a time
For it fills me with immense joy
*To be known, as "**The Olive Wife**".*

The Greatest Fashionista

The devil wears Prada
And me Vero Moda
For I am the queen
The goddess of style
The greatest fashionista
You, will ever find

My closet is over flowing
My wardrobe bursting at its seams
There is a party in the evening
But I don't have anything to wear
Can't you see?

Got my Ferrari out of the garage
And sped towards the nearest boutique
Where I would be served tea in China
And made to feel I was a diva,
Spending a day, like in Tiffany's

Got myself, not just a chiffon dress
But Swarovski crystal studded heels
And a matching tiara to adorn my head

Isn't that enough????? My husband called
and asked me to stop
And just coz he said that,
Got myself a diamond watch

Came home, showered, powdered my nose
and got dressed
Anticipating all the attention, that I was
about to get

Phew! What a life I have
Being a shopaholic isn't that bad
My fashion statements are to say, the very
best
So come to me, when you are in doubt and
distress
Coz in my wardrobe, I will find you, the
best dress.

A Midnight Date

In the middle of the night
When I wake up all alone
Crickets are chirping
And owls are hooting
I look outside my window
And see the moonlight streaming through the trees
Hoping to catch, a glimpse of me
As I play a little hide and seek

Just as it was about to give up
Losing hope of ever seeing me
I open the window
And invite it right in

How I wish you were here
To hold me close and share the wondrous moment
We could have conversed the whole night long
Gazing out of the window
With the moonlight streaming along

Your voice...alluring and bewitching
Crooning in my ears
As we would steal a midnight kiss
The moon would glide along our silhouette
Capturing an amorous moment
To be framed and kept on my bedside

So the next time I wake up in the middle
of the night
I will know, that I am not alone
But with you, always by my side.

Beautiful You

What a beautiful soul you have
What a beautiful face
A charming grace
Beautiful taste
In everything that you ever say

You never go unnoticed, whenever you enter the room
But what you are always looking for
Is the one, who called out to you

Like an angel sent from above
You walk in and lay your eyes
On the one in the darkest corner
The one who needs, your light

You uplift the loneliest
You stand tall for the weakest
You wipe away the flowing tears
You bring only happiness and cheer

A touch of compassion, is what your hands
give
A hug full of warmth, only sunshine could
give
Comfort, only your presence could bring
And a calm, only your smile could bring.

One Starlit Night

I sat with you one starlit night
Up on the meadow
And wished upon the shooting star
As it completed its circle of life

I lay down and closed my eyes
On a carpet of yellow flowers
And fireflies, illuminating the dark sky
As if they were tiny delicate lights

There was some magic in the air
Like the stars were carrying secrets
Which they would rather not bare

We spoke of everything under the blanket of stars
Of you, me and the unknown tomorrow

A chuckle I heard and I turned towards the sound
Saw a little girl frolicking amongst the flowers
Calling me towards her and telling me it was about time
For she had been waiting for me
For such a long time...

Now that you are here
Sit down beside me and hold my hand.........

Those sweet little fingers, gently laced through mine
Her head on my lap and her eyes observing mine,
"You have been lost far too long
You need to now come back
For what you have left behind
Was never yours, so don't go back in time
Live in the present
Love the one by your side
It isn't worth it
So don't cry and waste your time"

She pecked my cheek, gave me a hug and pat my back
And I found myself beside you
In your gentle embrace
Where I have always, felt right.

Intertwined Lives

As I watched the sunset
Its breath-taking hues splash all over the evening sky
I sat on the highest mountain peak
Thinking of my life, as it was passing by

I sat crossed legged picking up small stones
Drawing a little design on the earth below
Those tiny yellow flowers, dancing in the wind
And pale yellow butterflies, trying to flutter their wings
I looked up at the sky and saw it change its colour
What once was golden, was turning into a striking crimson

In the blink of an eye, behind the clouds
I saw the sun set
Who was eagerly waiting to be the sunrise
For the little girl, sleeping soundly in her bed

As he streamed his first rays of gold on her sweet innocent face
She woke up with a feeling, that someone was watching her
From the mountain top afar

Indeed our lives are intertwined they both thought
For one needed the white shimmery moon along with the stars
While the other, basked in the glory of a bright sunny day
Thinking of how today, was going to be, the most amazing day.

In Search of Home

It is in your arms
In your embrace
That I found
What I had been searching for

It is in your eyes
On your lips
That I found
What I had been yearning for

It is in your touch
In your love
That I found
What I had been pining for

A safe haven
A place to call my own...
With you I found me
My destination
And I could stop wandering
Knowing I was finally...home.

Rebellion

They worshipped her during the day
Singing her songs
With devotion and praise
And yet...
In their own homes
Insignificant is what she was
A slave to their whims and fancies
A foot mat at their doorstep
She had to prove her worth, every single
day
So she went ahead and got herself inked
In Mahamritunjay.

I Saw Death!!!

I saw death the other day
Lurking in the corner
Pouncing, on whoever came its way
Young or old
Man, woman or child
It did not matter
As long as it satiated its hunger
Like a wild beast
Roaming free, unruly, uncouth
It devoured just about everything
Even its own shadow

I walked up quietly
As it roamed about
Trying to figure out
What next, to quench its thirst

Everything seemed gloomy and dull
Only a pall of gloom, stood out
Grey skies
Screeching birds
Ear shattering cries
And flowing tears

Feeling my presence
Death looked at me
Gave a smirky smile
Telling me, it was my time

As I stared back intently
Death wondered, what was wrong with me
I just stood
Without batting an eyelid
For I knew,
This was just a dream

The tables turned soon enough
As the wind chased death away
It cried a howling wail
For it was not allowed, to take me away

As the dark clouds gave way to a new day
New leaves blossomed
The sun shone bright
The birds sung a mellifluous melody
And I, joined in
Knowing in my heart
That I am, meant to be.

Musings of My Heart

There was so much I wanted to say
When you said good bye
Left me all alone
And looked the other way

I kept waiting for the doorbell to ring
So I could run and be in your arms
And be happy
Bursting with joy, and feeling new again

I waited for hours, then days and months
But you never came
And there I stood...in the dark...feeling lonely and miserable
Waiting to feel alive and breathe again

Out of the blue, I found myself in the spotlight
The violin serenading the empty theatre
Pushing me to the edge of the cliff
Asking me to take a leap of faith
To believe in myself

I choked on my own breath
Scared...trying to flee and hide

Something snapped in me
And I found myself, wanting to feel alive
So...I flew...scaling new heights
Looking at the wondrous views
Soaring high as the applause grew
Never to return
Only looking at the horizon, as it beckoned me
Like a mother, beckons her child

As I neared my destination
I could not contain my joy
For what I saw, took my breath away
And happy tears welled up in my eyes

I saw you waiting
All decked up, looking at me
And that is when I knew,
I belonged with you

Swaying to empyreal tunes, in each other's arms
Heaven...like sweet nectar,
Nothing more, nothing less
Surrounded by our love
Celebrating each other
From dawn, until dusk.

Circle of Life

As the last leaf fell off the tree
It lay blissfully
On the ground beneath
And heaved, a sigh of relief

Not out of sadness but peace
For it had lived a wholesome life
From being a tiny leaf, turning into a beautiful hue, of orange and green

It had been witness to so many events
Some happy moments, some tragedies
Some unshed tears some innocent fears
Of children running around
Of the elders trying to make it about,
Or the tired worker who sat under its shade
Having a sip of water, after a long, tiring day

Many a kids marvelled at the leaves
Some plucked them because they wanted to feel
How soft they felt to touch,
How they beautifully smelled...
A few kept them in their books

To see how they were changing,
Of what remained, was their true being

A beautiful life, that's what the leaf had
It weathered the sun, the rain, the wind and the cold
Fluttering to a divine music
It was humming within

As the days, weeks, months and years passed
It smiled merrily and danced to the tune of life
Enjoying each moment, each tug, each pull
And what it got, was an unbelievable encore

So as it breathed its last breath
Slowly and softly making its way to Mother Earth,
To lay still in her arms
As she welcomed it home, turning it into golden dust

To be reborn again
In times to come
On a warm spring day
And open its eyes,
To see the marvel, that is life, all over again.